digging deeper **1** BRITAIN 1066-1500

ALAN BROOKS-TYREMAN   JANE SHUTER   KATE SMITH

Heinemann

Heinemann Educational Publishers
Halley Court, Jordan Hill, Oxford, OX2 8EJ
a division of Reed Educational & Professional Publishing Ltd
Heinemann is a registered trademark of Reed Educational & Professional Publishing Ltd

OXFORD MELBOURNE AUCKLAND
JOHANNESBURG BLANTYRE GABORONE
IBADAN PORTSMOUTH NH (USA) CHICAGO

First published 2000

ISBN 0 435 32771 2

02 01 00
10 9 8 7 6 5 4 3 2 1

Designed and produced by Gecko Limited, Bicester, Oxon

Original illustrations © Heinemann Educational Publishers 2000

Illustrated by Mike Spoor

Printed and bound in Spain by Mateu Cromo

Picture research by Diana Philips

Photographic acknowledgements
The authors and publisher would like to thank the following for permission to reproduce photographs:
Bibliotheque National, Paris: 46A, 53C
Bodleian Library: 57C, 58E, 60C
Bridgeman Art Library: 20A, 40A
British Library: 27E, 29B, 32E, 35A, 37B, 38A, 39E, 50A, 52B, 61D
British Museum: 12E
Durham Cathedral: 49D
Fotomas: 59A, 62E
Michael Holford: 6A, 8A, 9B, 42A, 44C, 45D, 55A
Trinity College, Cambridge: 31B, 48C

Cover photograph: British Museum

The publisher has made every effort to trace the copyright holders, but if they have inadvertently overlooked any, they will be pleased to make the necessary arrangements
at the first opportunity.

Written sources acknowledgements
The authors and publishers gratefully acknowledge the following publications from which written sources in the book are drawn. In some sources the wording or sentence has been simplified.

D. Birt, *The Norman Conquest*, Longman, 19XX: 7B, 7C
C. Culpin, *Medieval Realms 1066–1500*, Collins Educational, 1991: 4A, 7D, 10B, 17B, 18E, 18H, 18I
C. Dyer, *Everyday Life in Medieval England*, Hambledon Press, 1994: 26B, 27F, 27G, 15D
N. Kelly, *Medieval Realms*, Heinemann Educational, 1995: 10A, 17C, 17D, 18F, 18G
N. Kelly, R. Rees and J. Shuter, *Living Through History: Roman Empire and Medieval Realms*,
Heinemann Educational 1997: 4B
J. Mason, *Medieval Realms*, Longman, 1991: 17A
A. Murray, *Medieval Christmas* in *History Today*, Vol. 36, 1986: 40B
J. Nichol and D. Downton, *Evidence – The Middle Ages*, Blackwell: 20A, 21B
C. Reeves, *Pleasures and Pastimes in Medieval England*, Sutton, 1995: 38D
M. Rosen (ed.), *The Penguin Book of Childhood*, Viking, 1994: 60B
J. L. Singman and W. McLean, *Daily Life in Chaucer's England*, Greenwood Press, 1995: 26A, 26C, 38C
J. Stow, *Survey of London*, Everyman, 1965: 38B

CONTENTS

HISTORICAL SKILLS

DIGGING DEEPER

THEMES

Primary and secondary sources – medieval times

Since the medieval period was so long ago we cannot ask people who lived then what their lives were like. We have to piece the story together using as many sources of evidence as we can. Fortunately there are a lot left to help our enquiry into what happened in medieval times.

Secondary sources

The quick route for finding out about the past is to use a secondary source. This is a previous study of the past like your text book or an historian's account. In this way you can gain a great deal of information from research that has already been done for you, but you are going to have to rely on what other historians say. They may not have got it right!

Primary sources

Using primary sources takes longer. These are sources from the time we are studying. They may be written sources or pictorial sources or artefacts (things made by people in the past). When you look at primary sources you are not depending on what other historians have said. But you have to be careful. Primary sources can still be inaccurate. Just because things were written down or made at the time doesn't make them accurate.

Source A is a primary source describing what happened to the English after the Norman invasion. It was written by English monks in *The Anglo Saxon Chronicle* for 1087. This chronicle (account of the past) was a diary that was written once a year by several different writers. Source B is a secondary source from a modern school history book.

SOURCE A

Alas, what a miserable and sorry time it was. The people were nearly driven to death and there was a terrible famine which completely destroyed them.

King William and his followers were greedy for gold and silver. They didn't care what methods they used as long as they got it. The Normans charged high rent for land and took unfair taxes. They did countless other illegal things.

SOURCE B

The English did not always accept their new Norman lords without a fight – especially when taxes were put up. An important rebellion took place in the north. With the help of a large force sent by the King of Denmark, English rebels burnt William's castle in York to the ground. William defeated the rebels and destroyed villages, farms and livestock across a wide area. This caused terrible famine and many people died of starvation.

Work it out!

1 Study Source A and make a list of the complaints against the Normans.

2 a Read the information about the source and Source B. What would make you doubt that everything in Source A is accurate?

  b What is there in Source B that helps you to believe Source A?

3 What problems might an historian have with:

- secondary sources
- primary sources?

Explain your answers.

Using evidence – the Norman Conquest

In 1066 England was invaded by a Norman army led by Duke William. Below is a list of events that happened in 1066 leading up to the Battle of Hastings. Draw a larger timeline like the one on the page and put the events into the correct order of time (this is called chronological order).

14 October 1066 **The Battle of Hastings**. The English army was defeated by the Normans.

6 January 1066 **Death of Edward the Confessor**. Edward had no children to succeed him. Before he died he named Harold Godwinson his heir.

25 September 1066 **Battle of Stamford Bridge**. Harold Godwinson defeated another claimant to the throne, Harald Hardrada, and his Viking army at this battle.

30 September 1066 **William's army landed in England**.

28 September 1066 **William set sail**. 696 ships left the ports of Normandy to cross the Channel to England.

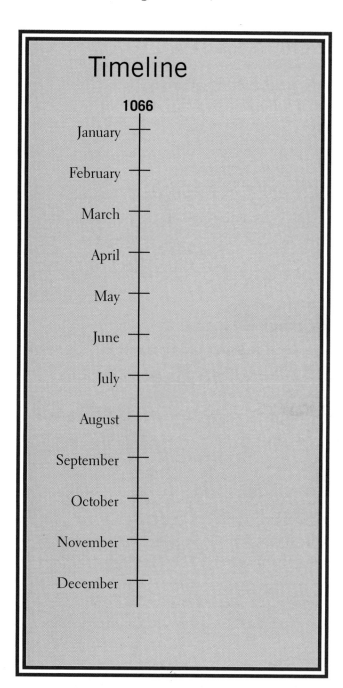

Timeline

1066

January
February
March
April
May
June
July
August
September
October
November
December

The Bayeux Tapestry

The most famous source is the Bayeux Tapestry. It is like a huge strip cartoon telling us about the events that led to William the Conqueror becoming King of England. It is about 0.61 metres wide and 70.10 metres long. The Bayeux Tapestry was produced in Normandy by English nuns and was finished by 1077. It was commissioned (ordered) by Bishop Odo of Bayeux, William the Conqueror's brother, who had been at the battle.

Work it out!

1 Look at Source A.

   a Make a list of all the things you can see in the picture.

   b From your list, try to work out what is happening.

   (For example, what do you think is the importance of the axes? How can we tell who the man on the right is? What is he doing?)

   c Reading the Latin will also help: (on the left) 'Here they gave Harold the King's crown.' (On the right) 'Here sits Harold, King of the English, beside him, Archbishop Stigand.'

2 You have looked at the source, read the information (so you know who produced the tapestry and when) and tried to work out what is happening. Now explain:

   a whether you think this source is likely to be accurate.

   b whether you would like to find other primary evidence to help you to decide.

SOURCE A

A scene from the Bayeux Tapestry showing Harold immediately after the death of Edward.

Other sources from the time

One of the problems with history is that it is usually the people who win the battles who write the history. They have the power and decide how they wish to be remembered once the losers are dead! So it would not be fair to look at only one source, the Bayeux Tapestry, to decide what happened in 1066. We need to look at what other people have said.

SOURCE B

An unwelcome report arrived that King Edward had died and that Harold had been crowned King. This wicked man Harold did not wait to be chosen, he broke his promise to William and with a few evil supporters seized the throne on the day of King Edward's funeral when everyone was in mourning.

Written by William of Poitiers in about 1071. He was a Norman soldier who became a priest and worked for William of Normandy for most of his life. He praised his leader in his book *The deeds of William, Duke of the Normans and King of the English*.

SOURCE C

Harold seized the Kingdom, breaking his oath to the Duke William who sent messages to Harold telling him to stop this mad attempt and keep his promises.

William of Jumièges wrote this in *The deeds of the Dukes of Normandy* around 1070. He was a Norman monk.

SOURCE D

Angels led the soul of King Edward to heaven. This wise King had given his Kingdom to Harold because he was a great nobleman. He had always been loyal and trustworthy. He had carried out all the King's orders and done everything that was needed.

This was written in Latin by English monks in *The Anglo Saxon Chronicle*. It was written at the time of the Conquest.

The Bayeux Tapestry, William of Poitiers and William of Jumièges give the Norman side of the story. *The Anglo Saxon Chronicle* gives the English side of the story.

Work it out!

1 You will need to know that according to the Bayeux Tapestry Harold had promised to support William's claim to the throne of England.

   a Look at what William of Poitiers and William of Jumièges had to say. List the words that suggest to you that they were Normans and were against Harold's claim to the throne.

   b Why do you think they might have written these accounts?

2 a What impression do we get of Harold from Sources B and C?

   b What impression do we get of Harold from Source D?

3 Do you think that there are any reasons why we might believe any one of these accounts more than the others?

4 What do these sources show us in the way of problems that we may find when we try to use primary sources?

Finding out what happened at the Battle of Hastings

Fact file of the Battle of Hastings

- Harold and his army had fought and won the Battle of Stamford Bridge only 18 days before the Battle of Hastings. They had lost many soldiers. They had marched 190 miles (306 km) south to meet William, who had landed in England the day after Stamford Bridge.

- Harold had about 7000 soldiers, but they were exhausted, and he had few archers and horsemen.

- William had about 7000 soldiers, including many archers and horsemen.

- Harold cleverly positioned his army on the top of a hill surrounded by marsh land so that the Normans would have to climb to high ground to fight. This would put them at a disadvantage.

- William sent out scouts during the night to look for the English. His soldiers surprised the English early in the morning.

- At first the Norman knights could not break through the English shield wall. They were pushed down the hill.

- There was a rumour that William was dead. The Normans retreated. The English charged down the hill, but William rallied his soldiers and turned his men to face the English. Now the battle was on more equal ground, and the fighting was hard. And then Harold was killed, and his men deserted to the Normans.

SOURCE A

A scene from the Bayeux Tapestry showing the height of the battle. According to the Bayeux Tapestry, 'many Norman and English soldiers fell together'.

This scene from the Bayeux Tapestry shows Harold being killed (this is what *Harold rex interfectus est* means). There are several men dying in this picture, but which is Harold?

Work it out!

1 Describe with as much detail as you can what you see in Source A. Does this source give a good idea of what fighting in 1066 was like?

2 Who might have expected to win the Battle of Hastings?

In order to try to answer this question, start by reading the Fact file.

Copy the boxes below and list the information in the story under the following headings:

	Harold	William
Advantages		
Tactics to try to win		
Disadvantages		
Mistakes		

Using the chart, write an account of the battle that shows that the English could have won, and then write another showing that the Normans deserved to win. The fact that the Normans won the battle does not necessarily mean that they deserved to win it.

Using a writing frame – medieval medicine

It is important to understand the difference between our own lives and past times. Read the following secondary source written in 1997 in a text book about health and medicine. Look for differences between medieval life and our own.

Nobody really understood what caused ill health. Some people thought that it was just bad luck while others blamed the position of the planets. There was a belief at the time that the body was made up of four humours or fluids and if these got out of balance, illness occurred.

It was very dangerous to undergo surgery. There were no operating theatres and the surgeon knew nothing about germs and so he wore his ordinary clothes and did not even wash his hands. Surgeons may have had another job such as barbers or butchers and, therefore, had knowledge of how to use a knife! They could generally successfully pull out teeth and mend fractures but tended to fail when they had to cut deeper or amputate. They sometimes used opium to put the patient to sleep. Surgery improved during medieval times because surgeons could learn from helping the injured soldiers on the battlefield.

Drug and 'sand bag' the patient unconscious, tie up securely: If you must cut, do so boldly: loss of blood is less, the shock minimised (lessened).

An extract from a book called *The Art of Medicine and Surgery*, written in 1412 by John Arderne.

Work it out!

Writing frames are designed to help you build up a piece of extended writing by giving you guidance on what to put in each paragraph. Use the writing frame below to write what you know about the differences between our understanding of ill health and surgery and medieval ideas. The writing frame has divided your answer into four sections.

1 These days, we believe that ill health is caused by ....

   (Mention: germs, housing, pollution, smoking, poor diet and lack of exercise.)

2 In medieval times, people believed that illness was caused by ....

   (Mention: bad luck, the planets and humours.)

3 Today we expect surgeons to know more than how to use a knife ....

   (Mention: cleanliness, knowledge, anaesthetic, experience, operating equipment and blood transfusions.)

4 In medieval times, surgery was very dangerous.............

   (Mention: ordinary clothes, dirt, ignorance about germs, blood loss, putting the patient to sleep and experimenting on the battlefield.)

Testing the reliability of sources – life in the monasteries

Historians use a variety of evidence in their studies. Part of their task is to piece together what has happened from a number of sources. One thing they have to be careful about is whether they can believe everything the sources say or show. Sources that can be believed are called reliable. On these pages there are five sources from medieval times giving us information about life in the monasteries. It is your aim to work out how reliable you think they all are.

Introduction

Some men and women made the decision to become monks or nuns and lived in a monastery or convent. Strict rules had to be followed. Many monasteries followed the Rules of St Benedict, whose monks, led by St Augustine, founded the first monastery in England at Canterbury in 597. They were not allowed to own any possessions (poverty), they had to do as they were told (obedience) and they could not have sexual relations (chastity). They had to live a holy life.

However, not everybody followed these rules.

SOURCE A

Dame Isabel Benet and Agnes Halesley, nuns of Catesby, will not obey the orders of the bishop. Also the same Dame Isabel spent last Monday night with the Friars of Northampton. She danced and played the lute with them until midnight.

Extract from a fourteenth century book called *A Visitation of Religious Houses*.

SOURCE B

A monk there was, one of the finest sort
Who rode the country; hunting was his sport.
A manly man, fit to be an Abbot
He had many dainty horses in his stable.
The Rule of good St Benedict
As old and strict he tended to ignore.
Greyhounds he had, as swift as birds to run.
Hunting a hare or riding at a fence
Was all his fun, no matter what the expense.

From Geoffrey Chaucer's poem *The Canterbury Tales* written in the 1380s.

Others did follow the rules.

SOURCE C

We have little food, our clothes are rough, our drink is from the stream and our sleep often upon our book. Under our tired bodies is but a hard mat; when we are fast asleep a bell is rang to wake us. There is no moment to be idle or play. We have peace of mind and a marvellous freedom from the hurly burly of the world.

Extract from *The Monastic Order of England*. This was by Ailred of Rievaulx, who wrote about his life as a monk in about 1135.

- All monks shall take turns to wait on each other so that no one is excused kitchen work.

- Above all, care must be taken of the sick.

- Laziness is the enemy of the soul. Monks should be busy working or reading holy books.

- A mattress, woollen blanket and pillow is enough for bedding.

Some of the Rules of St Benedict.

SOURCE E

This painting shows a cellarer. He was the monk who had the keys to the wine cellar. It comes from an illuminated manuscript produced in the 13th century. Some monasteries were famous for making good wine.

SOURCE REPORT

Source description ....
Written/drawn by ....
Date ....

List of reasons to doubt source
1 ....
2 ....
3 ....
....

List of reasons to believe source
1 ....
2 ....
3 ....
....

Do other sources support it?

Source A
  support? ....
  ....
  ....
  oppose? ....
  ....
  ....

Source C
  support? ....
  ....
  ....
  oppose? ....
  ....
  ....

Source D
  support? ....
  ....
  ....
  oppose? ....
  ....
  ....

My view on the reliability of this source ....

Work it out!

1 Read Source A. What has Dame Isabel done wrong?

2 Look at Source B. Which of the three rules of obedience, chastity and poverty has the monk broken?

3 Read Sources C and D and make a chart with a set of rules by which monks should live.

4 Look carefully at Source E and describe in detail what you see.

   a What do you think the monk is doing in the picture?

   b Do you think he could be trusted to look after the cellar?

   c What do you think the artist is trying to say?

5 Which of the five sources tells us most about being a monk or nun? Give reasons for your answer.

Can we trust our sources?

Your answers to questions 1–5 were based on Sources A to G and the assumption that they were telling you 'correct' history. Supposing you were told that the monk who wrote Source C was really miserable and hated his life as a monk. That would be bound to affect what you thought about his account because it might be unreliable.

Look at Source B. This is a poem written at the time that you are studying. We are going to look at this poem and try to work out how reliable we think it is.

Sources may be *unreliable* for many different reasons:

Reasons to doubt Source B

Chaucer might be just trying to tell a good story, and was worried about whether his poem was accurate.

This might be a description of only one monk. Other monks may have lived a godly life. Chaucer might have put in words just to get the rhythm of his poem to work.

Chaucer might have been one of the growing number of people who were starting to criticise the weaknesses of people in the Church. So he could be biased.

Reasons to believe Source B

Chaucer may have known this monk.

The monk that he is describing might have been typical of many monks in the monasteries.

Chaucer lived at the time and so he may have seen people like this.

Chaucer was well educated and had great power with words. His description is likely to be accurate.

6 a Would you say that Chaucer was praising or criticising the monk in this passage? Use the detail in the poem to support your answer.

   b Now we need to ask: Can we accept this source as evidence we can believe - ie is it *reliable*? Support your answer by using the reasons above.

One way that we can test the reliability of a source is to look at whether other sources support it. This means it is likely to be reliable but does not prove it.

7 Copy and complete the **Source Report** for each of the other four sources. Allow space for your reasons. Note that this report is for Source B.

Testing sources – medieval manuscripts

Before the invention of the printing press, books had to be hand written. They were produced by monks who wrote in Latin and are called manuscripts. The books were very precious because they took a long time to produce. Often one monk did the writing and another illustrated the work. They tended to be a history of the monastery, part of the Bible or a prayer book. Sometimes the monk described what had happened during his lifetime.

These manuscript sources are important in helping us to find out about the past. But we must not take them at face value. We must consider their strengths and their weaknesses as historical sources:

- Writing by hand was very slow.
- We sometimes learn about important events – like the murder of Becket.
- Monks may have heard rumours, or been told first hand accounts from travellers and visitors.
- Monks may not have known much about life outside the monastery.
- Manuscripts were written in Latin, so only the educated could read them.
- Manuscripts may make out that religion was more important than it really was.

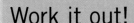

An illuminated manuscript dating from about ten years after the murder of Thomas Becket. On the right is Becket's shrine, where pilgrims sat to be close to his body.

Work it out!

1 From your knowledge of Becket's murder explain what you can see in Source A.

2 Do you think such a detailed illustration for this Latin account of the murder would have been a help to the readers?

3 Write out the points above and explain whether each one is describing a strength or a weakness or both.

4 Explain how useful you think medieval manuscripts are to historians.

Testing the usefulness of sources – how do we find out about women's lives in medieval times?

We want to find out about how women lived in medieval times. How easy is it? This may depend on how useful the sources are.

SOURCE A

Taken from a medieval book called a Bestiary which told stories about animals.

SOURCE B

The peasant woman managed the family and worked for a living. It was her job to make sure that what little money the family had was spent wisely and that there was enough food to eat. Her diet was mainly bread with a little cheese. She also made soup for her family from vegetables which she grew herself. She worked in the fields alongside her husband, spun wool, kept a few chickens and milked the cows. She married for life, and a good wife produced as many children as possible!

An extract from a modern history book written in 1999.

SOURCE C

Rich women normally had servants to run their households, but they were expected to defend their homes if their husbands were not there. If a woman's husband was away at war, his work had to be done as well. Some who were less well off had to earn a living by spinning wool or making cloth; others would work on the land with their husbands.

A secondary source from a modern history book.

SOURCE D

A woman is a worthy thing
They do the wash and do the wring
Lullay, Lullay she doth sing
And yet she hath but care and woe
A woman is a worthy sight
She serveth man both day and night
Thereto she pulleth all her might
And yet she hath but care and woe.

From a medieval song.

SOURCE E

Women spinning, carding and weaving. A French painting from the 15th century.

1 Your task is to decide which sources are most useful in finding out about women's lives during medieval times.

Judging usefulness

When you try to find out how useful a source is, you will need to ask some questions:-

- *Who* produced the source?

- Do we know *why* it was written, or produced?

- *When* was the source written/drawn?

- *What* can we learn from the source?

2 Look at the box 'Judging usefulness' and ask each of the questions about each of the Sources A-E. Write your answers on a chart copied from the one here.

3 Now use the chart you have made to help you answer the question 'Which source gives us the most information about women's lives?'

	Source A	Source B	Source C	Source D	Source E
Who made it?					
Why?					
When?					
What can we learn?					
How useful is it?					

Using evidence – the Black Death: symptoms and cures

The Black Death arrived in England in June 1348. It was said to have been brought over by a French soldier suffering with the plague. Between 1347 and 1349 it killed one in three people in Europe. Nobody knew what caused it or how to avoid it.

We now know that it was really two types of plague. One affected the lungs, and the other was the bubonic plague, which caused the victim to break out in boils. Both caused rapid death.

The bubonic plague was spread by fleas which lived in the hair of rats. At that time, people did not understand about germs or hygiene and they were rather dirty. Towns were overcrowded and the streets often full of sewage and rubbish (and rats) which encouraged disease. In the villages rats lived in the thatched roofs and rubbish heaps.

There are many colourful descriptions from the time of the Black Death written by people from different countries in Europe. In their writings, medieval people described the symptoms of the plague, tried to work out the causes of the disease and suggested remedies. From these written sources historians try, with modern knowledge, to work out what were the symptoms, and what were the causes of the plague.

Symptoms and reasons for the Black Death

SOURCE A

In men and women alike it first showed itself by the appearance of swellings in the groin or armpits. Some grew as large as an apple or an egg. From these two parts of the body this deadly swelling soon began to spread. Then black spots began to appear on the arms or thigh.

Written by Boccaccio in 1351 in his introduction to *The Decameron*, a book of collected stories. Boccaccio was an Italian romantic writer who witnessed the plague in Florence in 1348.

SOURCE B

Woe is me of the shilling in the armpit. It is a white lump that gives pain. It is like an apple, like the head of an onion, a small boil that spares no one. It burns like a cinder.

Getlin, a Welsh writer, describes the various symptoms of the Black Death, 1349.

SOURCE C

Saturn, Jupiter and Mars are close to each other. It is always a sight of terrible things to come.

Written by a 14th century French doctor.

SOURCE D

God has sent the plague to our town because the people spend so much time gambling, fighting and attending tournaments.

The views of a 14th century citizen of Leicester, in England.

Cures

Toads should be dried in the sun and they should be laid on the boil. The toad will swell and draw out the poison of the plague into its own body. When it is full it should be thrown away and another toad applied to the boil.

An example of a doctor's advice to some of the plague victims.

Some tried drinking vinegar or bleeding themselves. Patients were given medicines containing anything from crushed rocks to insects.

Some medical remedies for people suffering from the plague.

You are to make sure that all the human excrement and other filth lying in the streets of the city is removed. You are to make sure that there are no more bad smells for people to die from.

Instructions issued by King Edward III to the Lord Mayor of London in 1349.

Many died in the streets and the death of those at home was usually only discovered by neighbours because of the smell of their rotting corpses. Bodies lay all over the place.

Boccaccio – introduction to *The Decameron*, 1351.

People were so terrified of the plague that brothers abandoned each other and wives even deserted their husbands. Worse still, parents refused to nurse their children acting as though they were nothing to do with them.

Boccaccio – introduction to *The Decameron*, 1351.

An illustration showing victims of the plague being buried in the town of Tournai in the Netherlands, 1349.

Work it out!

1 **a** Read Sources A and B. Write your own description of the symptoms of the plague.

   b Source A was written by an Italian and Source B was written by a Welshman. Look at the two sources and find clues to suggest that they are describing the same plague.

2 Sources C and D give two explanations of the causes of the Black Death.

   a Do you think the people at the time would have accepted them as valid reasons?

   b Do you accept them? Give reasons for your answer.

3 Read Sources E, F and G. Which cures do you think would be most successful and why?

4 Sources H, I and J describe what happened in Italy and Holland. Are they useful to historians studying the plague in England? Explain your answer.

Causation – the Peasants' Revolt

In 1381 in south-east England there were riots and rebellions which have been called ever since the Peasants' Revolt. Some of the causes had been developing for a long while beforehand, these are called *long-term causes*. Events that led up to the revolt are called *short-term causes*.

Copy the causes, cut them out and sort them into two groups: long-term causes and short-term causes. You may want first to put the cards into the order the events happened.

SOURCE A

John Ball leading his army towards London. An illustration from *The Chronicles* of Jean Froissart, who was a French traveller. These accounts cover stories of events from 1325 to 1400.

The Black Death (1348-49) had killed so many people that there was a shortage of labourers. The peasants who were left were in a strong position to ask for higher wages and shorter working hours.

The Statute of Labourers was introduced in 1351 following the Black Death. It stated that every man and woman should only receive the same wages as before the Black Death. The peasants were very angry about this.

On 30 May 1381 three tax collectors were murdered in Essex. The news was spread to Kent and Norfolk.

In the months leading up to the revolt, a poor priest called John Ball, started preaching against the wealth and power of the leaders of the Church and the landowners. He became so popular with the poor that he was put in prison.

King Richard decided to collect more tax in 1381 because the war was going badly. There were riots and some peasants refused to pay.

The king needed more money to pay for the war with France. In 1377, he introduced a Poll Tax. Everybody over the age of 15 had to pay.

Work it out!

1 Look at your two groups of causes. Which group gives the most important reasons for the Peasants' Revolt?

2 Explain if you agree or disagree with this statement:

'The main reason that the peasants decided to rebel was because they were asked to pay more tax.'

After the Black Death many peasants gained their freedom from their lords. Now they were less likely to obey their rulers.

Cross-referencing – what sort of man was Henry II?

Introduction

Henry II

Henry II ruled over much of France as well as England. He was constantly travelling from the borders of Scotland to the south of France to try to bring law and order to his kingdom. He reformed the system of royal justice. He gained control over the barons and strengthened the power of the crown. He reformed the system of royal justice, and wanted to lessen the power of the Church within his lands. He had hoped that Thomas Becket, as Archbishop of Canterbury, would help him to do this. Thomas Becket, however, upheld the rule of the Church. Although Henry was infuriated by this, he never intended Becket to die.

We are going to look at one primary source about Henry II and then read a second one to help us decide about the accuracy of the first.

SOURCE B

Our king is still red-faced, although old age and white hair have changed his colour a little. He is of average height. His head is a globe, as if the home of vast intelligence. When he is peaceful his eyes are clear, lack cunning and seem dove-like: when in a rage they gleam like fire and flash like lightening. As to his hair, he is in no danger of going bald. However, his head is closely cut. He has a broad, square, lion-like face. His feet are arched, and he has the legs of a horseman. A broad chest and muscled arms show him to be a strong, brave, busy man… although his legs are bruised and swollen from hard riding, he never sits down except on horseback or for meals…he always has his weapons at hand when not busy talking or with his books. When business and worries give him breathing space, he spends time reading, or with a group of priests trying to solve a difficult question.

Written by Peter of Blois, a priest at the court of Henry II.

In order to work out whether Peter of Blois, the author of Source B, is telling the truth about Henry II, historians try to find other evidence on the same subject and look for similarities (things that are the same) and differences. This is called *cross-referencing*.

Now look at Source C, which is from *The Chronicles* of Gerald of Wales.

Henry II, King of England, had a red, freckled face, a large, round head, grey eyes which glowed fiercely and grew bloodshot when angry, a fiery look and a harsh, cracked voice. His neck thrust somewhat forward from his shoulders, his chest was broad and square and his arms strong... In times of war, which often threatened, he gave himself barely a second of peace to deal with other government business. In times of peace he did not allow a moment's rest. Beyond belief was his keenness for hunting. At the crack of dawn he was off on horseback, crossing heaths, riding deep into forests and climbing mountains. So he passed restless days. On his return in the evening he was rarely seen to sit down before or after supper. His non-stop standing wore out his courtiers. He was very careful to protect and keep peace. In giving money to the poor he was generous beyond compare. Henry promised to defend the Holy Land. He loved the humble, condemned the proud and took care to keep the nobles in their place.

Gerald of Wales also wrote about Henry II shortly after his death in his *Chronicles* **(accounts of the past).**

Work it out!

1 **a** Read the two sources carefully and then copy and fill in the chart below with all the things that are similar in both Source B and Source C.

  b Now make a list of the different things that the sources mention.

2 If two sources give similar information, does this mean that

  a what they say must be correct

  b what they say is more likely to be correct

  c what they say is less likely to be correct?

Before you write an answer to this question, think about these points:

● Could one writer have copied another? (When were the sources written?)

● Could an author have written to please someone else (his employer, for example)?

● How do the differences between the sources help you to make a judgement?

3 Read the introduction. What can you find in the sources to help us to understand some of the events of Henry's reign?

4 Use both the sources to select information to describe Henry II. Use quotes and your own words. Make sure that you refer to his appearance, hobbies and interests, and personality.

	Appearance	Hobbies & Interests	Personality
Source B			
Source C			

Pilgrims, saints and miracles

In medieval times many people made pilgrimages, journeys to shrines, which are places associated with a particular saint or holy relic. Saints were ordinary people who had done something that made them special – most often dying for their beliefs in a spectacular way. The Church decided who was a saint and this decision could take many years. Bishop Anselm died in 1109. Requests to make him a saint began at once. He was not made a saint until 1720! It depended, in part, on how popular the shrine became and also how many miracles were reported there.

Miracles were what made a shrine popular. For, while people made pilgrimages for many reasons, most went hoping that the saint would cure them or their loved ones of an illness, or work some other miracle.

We are going to look at one of the most famous English shrines, that of St Thomas Becket in Canterbury. Archbishop Thomas Becket was murdered, hacked to death, in Canterbury Cathedral in 1170. The knights who did this believed they were carrying out the orders of King Henry II.

The first miracle was reported on the same day. The murder had been watched by monks and citizens, who had been too scared to intervene. Many of these watchers dipped their clothing in Becket's blood after the murder. One of these is said to have had a wife who was paralysed. He told her and various neighbours the story of the murder. His wife demanded that he soak the blood from his shirt into a cup of water. She drank this, and was (so it was said) instantly cured. Next day, a dying child was wrapped in Becket's bloodstained cloak and recovered. Four days later, after prayers to Becket, a cure was recorded in Gloucester, 170 miles (272 km) away.

SOURCE A

Becket's death was soon shown in books, paintings and even stained glass.

Profitable miracles

Miracles were very profitable. In 1198 the value of offerings at Thomas Becket's shrine was about £450 in money, jewels, cloth, wax candles, cripples' crutches, models of human limbs in wax and silver. This was an average yearly income. It could be more: in 1350 fear of the Black Death drove takings up to about £667, when an average worker's wage was about £3 a year.

The Canterbury monks buried Becket hastily, before the murderers could come back and dispose of the body. He was reburied in a tomb like this one, where pilgrims could crawl into the holes at the side to be close to the body.

News of the miracles spread quickly. People set off for Canterbury, each hoping for a miracle of their own. King Henry refused to believe the miracles and ordered the pilgrims to stop. Despite the fact that the cathedral was supposed to be closed, pilgrims sneaked in to pray, and accounts of miracles spread. Besides, it was not necessary to go to Becket's tomb for miracles to happen. There were reports of miracles from contact with cloth dipped in his blood or even from prayers to Becket. In 1174, a man in Rochester said he kept a town fire out of his home by waving a scrap of cloth dipped in Becket's blood. In 1173 Becket was made a saint; one of the quickest ever.

But Becket's miracles had a far wider reach. He was said to have cured an Icelander of toothache. A Frenchman who was being hanged called upon Becket to save him. The rope gave way, saving his life. A doctor with a bowel disorder was cured by Becket in a dream. Part of Becket's clothing, carried to Whitchurch, on the Welsh border, quickly produced over 20 miracles, most of them medical cures. Even places built in Becket's honour produced miracles.

The monks of Canterbury quickly compiled two huge books full of miracles told to them by pilgrims to the shrine – over 700 in the first 10 years. Although many pilgrims were ordinary people, the rich came too. Even Louis VII of France came to pray for Becket's help when his son and heir, Philip, was very ill. In 1174 Henry II finally made a public penance at the tomb, putting his head and shoulders inside the tomb and being whipped by a monk. The victory against the Scots that followed this penance was seen by many as another of Becket's miracles.

Work it out!

1 What was there about the site and method of Becket's death that made him a likely saint?

2 Why might people in the 12th century need to believe in miracles?

3 a What religious reasons might the Church have to encourage people to believe in saints and miracles?

  b What economic reasons might the Church have to encourage people to believe in saints and miracles?

Spending money in the 1450s

Wages rose and fell all through the medieval period, depending on how many workers there were and the demand for the work they did. There was an especially steep rise in the wages of labourers after the Black Death – the death of so many workers meant that those who survived could demand far better wages and working conditions, as they were in much greater demand. There were various laws about wages that give us the approximate earnings of various groups of people, but the amounts are still almost meaningless, unless we know more about what money was worth and what it was used for. They tell us, for instance, that craftsmen earned more than farm labourers and less than merchants. We could have worked this out by using common sense. We need to know more about the value of money at the time and about what people spent their money on.

Approximate yearly incomes in the 1450s

Type of person	Income
A lord	£10,000
A gentleman	£40-£1000
A merchant with a small business	£10
A farmer with his own farm and land	£10
A craftsman	£5
A farm worker	£4
A labourer	£2

These are the prices of new goods in a town market. (Note: 12 pennies (d) make one shilling (s) and 20 shillings make one pound (£).) Prices could vary a lot from place to place. City prices could be double that of prices in smaller towns. There was a steady trade in secondhand goods at local markets and fairs. We have no idea what a secondhand gown might cost, presumably it depended on the amount of wear it had had.

Average prices in the 1450s

Bible	£1-3		
ordinary book		2s	
a peasant's house, built	£3		
yearly rent for a craftsman	£1		
a cow		9s	
a horse	£2-3		
a carthorse	£1		
a sheep		1s	6d
a pig		3s	2d
a hen			2d
5 litres of good beer			$1\frac{1}{2}$d
5 litres of cheap beer			$\frac{1}{2}$d
2 loaves of rye bread			$\frac{1}{2}$d
2 loaves of white bread			2d
a leg of pork			4d
a roast pig			8d
10 eggs			1d
500 g butter			1d
500 g cheese			$1\frac{1}{2}$d
500 g wax candles		1s	
500 g animal fat candles			2d
a cap			7d
stockings		1s	8d
a townswoman's gown		4s	6d
a peasant woman's gown			9d
linen to make a shirt		1s	
shoes			6d

Work it out!

Look at the box on the previous page and answer these questions about John Smythe, a craftsman in Newcastle. He has a wife and two children. An apprentice lives with them, whom John must house, feed and dress. They have a small garden where they can grow vegetables and keep hens.

1 a How much money does John have left (in shillings) when he has paid the rent?

b How much does this give him to spend each week (in pence)?

2 John's first priority, rent paid, is food. He will need to buy 15 litres of cheap beer, 20 loaves of rye bread, 500 g of butter and 3 kg of cheese, to cover the family's basic needs. How much money does he have left now?

3 If he saves this money, how long would it take for him to afford:

a a leg of pork

b a gown for his wife

c 250 g of sugar

d shoes for his apprentice?

4 The wages and prices given in the tables you have used are both approximate. Does this mean that all the calculations you have just done are useless? Explain your answer.

Fish – a very important food

In the medieval period almost every town and village had a fish-pond. Manor houses and religious communities had their own private fish-ponds: some simple, some a complex system of dams, ponds and weirs. This seems to suggest that medieval people ate a great deal of fish. Why? Were they forced to? Did they just like the taste? Was everyone eating fish, or just some groups of people? What kinds of fish did they eat?

SOURCE A

The Church had 'days of penance', when people could not eat meat or, if strictly keeping the rule of the Church, animal produce such as eggs and cheese.

They could eat fish or shellfish. Fish days were every Wednesday, Friday and Saturday; the evening before important feast days and all through Lent. Most people followed the Church's rules most of the time.

From *Daily Life in Chaucer's England* written in 1995.

SOURCE D

A village mill, from a manuscript written and illustrated in the 14th century.

SOURCE B

Feast day	Fish day
0.5 cow	200 salt cod
1.5 calves	300 herrings
1 sheep	3 gallons (13.5 litres) of oysters
1 pig	3 conger eels
0.5 wild boar	whelks
2 kids	576 eels
6 chickens	5 smoked eels
12 pigeons	trout (no number)
450 eggs	salmon (no number)
	1 pickerel

Food for a royal family of eight and all their servants at King's Langley in 1290 on a feast day and a fish day. This ignores any bread, vegetables, fruit, herbs and spices or pastry used in the meals.

SOURCE C

2-3 lbs (1-1.5kg) of bread

3 pints (1.5 litres) of ale

vegetable stew

3oz (0.08kg) bacon or a herring (only some days)

An ordinary worker's daily food intake in about 1290.

This beautifully kept fish-pond appears in a Dutch 15th century painting of army encampments. Notice there is a sluice gate for draining the water, fenced off to preserve the fish.

SOURCE F

Freshwater fish, raised in ponds, were mainly eaten by the rich. While there is little evidence about the cost of starting a fishpond from scratch, we know that maintaining them was expensive. In 1444-5 John Brome of Baddesley Clinton had his fishponds enlarged, cleaned and re-stocked. It cost him almost £5. This would have paid the wages of a skilled builder for a year.

Well grown pond fish, such as pike, were so valuable that they were often given as presents, even among the rich.

From *Everyday Life in Medieval England* written in 1994.

SOURCE G

Herring (sea)	0.25d
Plaice (sea)	0.5d
Pike (river/pond)	12d
Pickerel (river/pond)	8d
Eel (river/pond)	1.5d

The price per fish of various fish in 1461. The price of fish went up and down, but they kept in proportion to each other, except when there was a sudden shortage or glut of one sort of fish.

Work it out!

1 What reason does Source A give for the importance of fish on the medieval menu?

2 How does Source B support this view?

3 Compare what the rich ate (Source B) with what ordinary workers ate (Source C). Did rich people go hungry on 'fish days'?

4 Read Source F. Why might only the rich have had fish-ponds?

5 Read Source G. Compare it with the fish in Source B. Name two fish that:

  a the rich family were most likely to have eaten;

  b the servants were most likely to have eaten.

6 a What sort of fish were poor people most likely to eat?

  b Was this a farmed fish?

  c How does Source D suggest another way for ordinary people to get fish, rather than buying them at market?

  d Can you think of another, simpler, way for poorer people to get fish?

John Reed – a medieval 'land developer'?

The Norfolk village of Rougham became a 'shrunken' village – one that during the 14th century became much smaller than it had been. Usually, when people try to explain why a village has shrunk, they can find few direct answers. The Black Death, changes in climate and crop failures were all behind the decline of many medieval villages. In the case of Rougham, however, we can place the blame more personally on the shoulders of a man called John Reed.

The Reed family until 1349

Before the Black Death hit Rougham in 1349, John Reed was a freeman farmer and his family was one of the four most important families in Rougham. The villagers grew enough crops for food for themselves and for their animals, but sheep farming was important from early in the medieval period, and became more so as the medieval wool trade expanded. John Reed kept sheep. We do not know much about John Reed's personal life, but we know that Reed married and had children. There are no records of the effects of the Black Death on Rougham, but Reed and his son Richard, at least, survived.

Changing fortunes

Reed's ancestors had been villeins, tied to the manor and the village. This would have been well known in the village – most families had lived there for many generations. For the Reeds to rise from villeins to freemen upset people, but it was not unknown; many villages had at least one family that did this. Reed's rise to lord of the manor was much more unusual. Such a jump in social position, at a time when people were expected to keep the God-given place they were born to, would have caused much resentment.

John Reed's rise

Reed began to take over more and more land in western Rougham. As he bought up pieces of land, Reed seems to have put more and more pressure on people with connecting pieces of land to sell to him. By 1379 Reed was lord of the manor. He was also involved in collecting the hated 1379 Poll Tax. The 1381 Poll Tax sparked off the Peasants' Revolt.

SOURCE A

After the Black Death there were far fewer people to work on the land. Those people demanded much better wages and conditions than before the Black Death.

Sheep farming needed fewer workers than growing crops.

The Peasants' Revolt

In 1381 the Peasants' Revolt broke out. The Norfolk peasants did not head for London, but set out to right wrongs closer to home. The biggest rising in Norfolk was in Rougham, and was an attack on Reed's house; over three quarters of the rioters were from Rougham itself – about half were tenants of Reed. One of them, Walter Aleyn, was under a lot of pressure from Reed to sell Reed his land. Several of them had sold their land to Reed, possibly because they needed the money and he pressured them to do so. Buildings were pulled down; much of the lead was taken from the roofs; doors and windows were broken. The rioters also stole many of Reed's possessions, including a cart, a millstone, several horses and a saddle, 16 pigs, and sacks of wheat, barley, malt and wool. The total value of Reed's losses were well over £50, when the peasants who caused the damage might have been earning between £1 and £3 a year.

Reed's response

In September 1381 Rougham manor court tried the local people (42 men and 5 women) who had been involved in the Peasants' Revolt. This court was run by Reed, yet most of the rebels were fined just 6d. A few of the better-off were fined 1s. Why was Reed not harder on them? The answer is simple. He needed them. He needed them as workers, for the manor still farmed crops in the fields. He also needed their co-operation. He had not finished his expansion and some of the rebels owned land that he wanted to buy. His tactics worked. He even got Walter Aleyn's land, although he had to trade him land on the other side of the village for it. By the time he died the area in Rougham to the west of the manor was almost all laid to pasture for Reed's sheep.

Work it out!

Write a speech about how unfair Reed has been in order to encourage the peasants as they organise the revolt, and then write Reed's response.

How did medieval people get rid of sewage?

An adult produces 1.3-1.5 litres of urine and 150-450 g of excrement each day. We do not think about the disposal problems this creates, because we have flushing toilets, drains and sewers which deal with the problem for us. In medieval times the problem was far more serious. All this sewage had to be moved. Medieval solutions to the human waste disposal problem varied, depending on where and when people lived.

Early castles

In the early medieval period (1066-1300), the solution in huge stone castles was garderobes: small rooms that jutted out over the walls with a hole covered by a seat. Castle builders tried to site garderobes over a stream or a moat, but this was not always possible. If not, the waste slid down the wall to the foot of the castle wall, or into a deep sewage pit. From here it was collected regularly by a servant called the 'gong farmer' (gong was a slang medieval word for toilet) and used as manure on the kitchen garden. Some castles had a garderobe on each level, one above the other, with a connecting drain running down the walls with an exit hole at the bottom. This was less draughty for the garderobe-user. However, the drains had to be quite big to prevent blockage and this made them big enough for a determined enemy to use as a route into the castle.

Carisbrooke Castle's keep, an early medieval building, had two garderobes which jutted out over the walls. The keep was up a steep flight of 70 stairs, so it was unlikely that its garderobes were the only toilets in later times!

Later castles

As castle living became more focused on comfort, more and more garderobes were built. By the end of the period many rich castle-dwellers used 'close stools' – chairs with a lidded section containing a removable pot or bucket that was emptied regularly by the servants. This was the solution, too, when wealthy people stopped living in castles and began living in large houses instead. The Normans had needed castles to keep control of the country they had invaded. As time passed there was less and less need for castles either against the Welsh or each other.

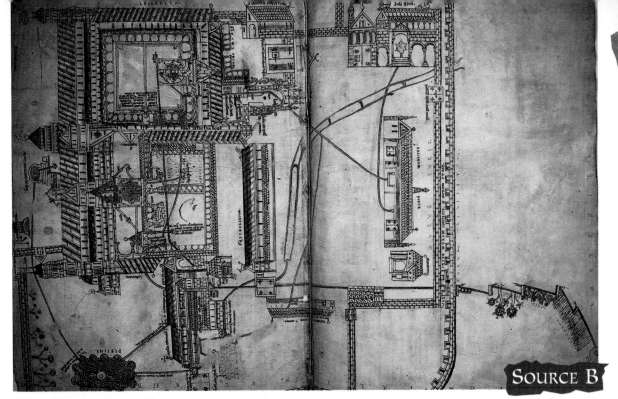

Water system for the monks of Canterbury, designed in 1153. The water pipes are shown in red.

Monasteries

Another wealthy group, that became richer all through the period, were religious communities of monks who lived in monasteries. Not all monasteries were wealthy. But the biggest of them were. Their monasteries, like castles, were built from stone. Some of them had their own complicated system of running water that provided everything from water for cooking to water to clear the drains that ran through purpose-built toilets. Throughout the period it was only in monasteries that toilets were kept clean by being part of a system with flowing water that flushed the waste away. This was partly because of the emphasis on cleanliness, and partly because a monastery was a single large community that could organise complete drainage throughout.

Peasants

Peasants who lived and worked in the countryside had very basic sewage arrangements, which did not change during the medieval period. They used an outdoor communal privy, which was emptied from time to time on to the fields, or they used a chamber pot in the house and emptied it directly on to the land. They often took a more direct approach, and used the fields themselves as a toilet. The law required that if they did this, they should be at least 'a bowshot' away from any houses.

Early town sewage

Towns grew enormously during medieval times. At the beginning of the period, rich and poor alike threw their rubbish and waste on to the streets or into the river. The river was seen as the better alternative, because the waste floated away; despite the fact that it was also the main water source. Big towns provided public toilets (London had several of these) which often had outlets on to the river.

31

Improved water and sewage

From 1200 on, some towns set up water supply systems. People paid to have water piped to their homes. At the same time, drains that took away 'waste' from kitchens and toilets alike were built. These, too, were provided only in some parts of some towns, for a yearly payment. The most common form of sewage disposal in the middle of the medieval period was the cesspit – a deep pit, often shared by several houses, that filled with sewage until it had to be emptied. The best cesspits were lined with stone, to prevent sewage seeping into the soil and contaminating the ground all around. Homes without access to drains or cesspits still threw their waste on to the streets. Most large towns employed 'raykers' to clean the streets and passed laws about dumping rubbish in the streets. This was only partly successful. Court cases show many raykers simply moved their rubbish into streets that had to be cleaned by other raykers.

Problems

Water provision and sewage disposal were very haphazard and could cause more trouble than they solved. The constant overflowing of water supply pipes in London so often flooded nearby houses that the owners paid for a 'vent pipe' to run off water. Cesspits were not always emptied as often as they should have been, and so overflowed, causing flooding of a more unpleasant kind.

The price of water

Water was an expensive commodity in medieval towns, especially fresh water from springs, rather than water from the polluted town river. Only the well-off could afford to have water piped to their homes. In the 1350s the water rate in Cheapside, London, was about 6s a year, about four weeks' wages for an ordinary worker.

SOURCE E

A water seller, from the 14th century Luttrell Psalter.

Cesspits

Cesspits remained the most common form of sewage disposal in the medieval period. Houses that had them, used them. Houses continued to be built with cesspits, either internal or attached to a separate 'seat house' in the yard. At the same time, sewage collection became more frequent.

Work it out!

1 What problems did medieval people face with sewage disposal?

2 a List as many medieval methods of sewage disposal as you can.

  b Choose one of these methods and outline its advantages and disadvantages.

3 'Medieval people just did not understand about the need for sewage disposal.' Do you agree? Explain your answer.

Do you know a good builder?

Castles and cathedrals

Many towns and cities today have great stone cathedrals and castles which were built in the early medieval period. They tell us how important religion and defence were to the medieval people and how skilled the craftsmen were to construct buildings that have survived so many years. But who did the building in medieval times?

A huge workforce

Large stone buildings needed many workers with various building skills. There were masons, carpenters, painters, plasterers and glaziers; all with various levels of skill. Labourers fetched and carried and did the heavy work. Away from the building site, workers quarried stone, chopped wood and transported it all to the site. In charge of everything was the master mason, who designed the building and organised deliveries, payment and work schedules.

A permanent workforce?

A castle or cathedral took years to build. Master masons were employed for the whole job, where possible. Most other workmen were employed on a weekly rate as they were needed. They were not employed, or paid, regularly from the end of September until the beginning of February. The weather at this time was too bad for building, although some indoor work could be done.

All good builders?

Good master masons were in great demand in medieval Europe. They worked in many different countries, and were seldom unemployed. Masons working on royal castles built several at once, travelling around as needed.

Others worked for different people at the same time; disputes often arose about where they should be working! A good master mason was important, because he was in charge of the entire project. If he made a mistake, the results could be disastrous and very expensive.

Buildings could, and did, fall down due to bad design or construction. In 960 an entire church at Evesham collapsed. More often, only parts of buildings gave way. Towers were especially likely to collapse, because of the extra weight of stone. These collapses were variously blamed on bad foundations (Gloucester, 1299), high winds (Dunstable, 1210) or the sinfulness of the person buried beneath it (Winchester, 1107).

Responsibility

The master mason had the best pay and working conditions, but he also had a huge responsibility. The balance between pay and responsibility went all the way down the line of workers – the master blacksmith was responsible for all the work done, whether he had done it himself or not. If a wall was not laid straight, the master layer was to blame. The most poorly paid people could work slowly or badly and hope not to be found out.

Wages

Wages varied through the Middle Ages, depending on the year, the demand for builders and prices. However, the wages for various groups kept the same pattern. Below are a sample of weekly wages paid to workers on castles in Wales in 1282.

Extras

The **master mason** was either given a place to live or money for rent. He was given money for food and clothing. Often he was promised a pension, even a pension to be paid to his family if he was killed on the site.

Craftsmen were given work clothes – gloves, leather aprons for blacksmiths – and were sometimes fed and housed.

Ordinary workmen were often just given beer and bread on their breaks. They often camped in and around the building site in summer.

In this painting, you can see the tools the builders had to work with. The thatched lodge in the background is where the builders worked in bad weather. Workers were sometimes expected to sleep and eat on the site in temporary buildings very similar to this, although they seldom lived in the lodge itself.

	Summer		Winter	
master mason	14s		14s	
quarriers		12d		
master layers (built the walls)	2s	4d	2s	
layer's assistant		14d		14d
carpenters		18d		
wood sawers		12d		
plasterers				9d
master blacksmiths	2s	4d	2s	
blacksmith's assistant		12d		12d
labourers		12d		9d

Ordinary homes

Very few ordinary medieval homes have survived. They were mostly made from wood and have, over the years, been affected by rot, fire and re-building. Building ordinary homes was a very different job from building a huge stone structure. Homes were made largely from wood and built by carpenters, working for themselves. They might employ several other carpenters and an apprentice or two, or just an apprentice, depending on the size of their business and the kinds of work they were given to do.

A medieval building contract

Summary of a contract between William Haute, knight, and John Brown, carpenter, for John Brown to build a row of four houses in St George's parish, by King Street, Canterbury, Kent. These were houses for craftsmen, so had workshops at the front of the house, with a flap that opened to the street and became a counter that the craftsman used to sell his goods.

Each house shall be 6.5 metres on the side facing the street and 6 metres back from the street.

Each house shall have:
- A workshop on the ground floor, facing the street: 3.5 m by 2.5 m.
- Behind the workshop, a buttery (for storing food and cooking and eating utensils): 2.5 m by 1.25 m.
- A hall behind the workshop with stairs leading to the room above.
- A kitchen (3 m by 3.5 m) behind the buttery, next to the hall.
- A garden or yard behind the hall.
- An upper room that juts out 0.5 metres all around. The upper floors touch, leaving a narrow passage between the houses at ground level.

William Haute must:
- clear the building site
- provide the wood and cart it to the yard where Brown will make the frames
- pay for the wood to be cut to length
- transport the framed wood to the building site.

John Brown must:
- provide a cart for moving the framed wood from his yard to the building site
- pay the wages of all the carpenters who work on the house building, as well as feed them and provide them with somewhere to live.

Finish time:
The work, including all doors and windows, is to be finished to William Haute's satisfaction by the Feast of St Michael (about seven months after the contract was made).

Payment:
William Haute will pay John Brown 20s in three instalments: on signing the contract, on finishing the framing and on finishing the houses.

If John Brown has paid out more than 20s, on things that were needed to complete the houses to Haute's satisfaction, Haute will pay enough to cover these costs.

Work it out!

1 a Which of the people on a medieval building site earned the most money?

b Which people earned the least money?

c How much was the difference in weekly wage between the lowest paid and the highest paid?

d In what other ways were the highest paid better off?

2 If you were going back in time to work on a medieval castle, would you rather be a master mason, a craftsman or a labourer? Think about:
- wages
- the work
- the level of responsibility.

Explain your answer.

3 a How, apart from size, were ordinary homes different from castles? List as many differences as you can.

b Who built ordinary homes?

4 a Looking at the contract between Haute and Brown, what costs would Brown's 20s have to cover?

b How could he save money?

c What problems might Brown meet if he did try to save money?

5 The description of the houses is unusually detailed for the time. Try to draw a plan, in scale, of the ground floor of one of the houses. Is there any other information you would need to be sure of the plan being exactly what Haute wanted?

In this painting, carpenters are building the frame for Noah's Ark. This is an illustration for a Bible story, but it shows how a timber frame for an ordinary house would have been put together, using lengths of wood held together with wooden pegs. The roof is being made from overlapping planks of wood, nailed to the frame. The painting also shows various carpentry tools. The saw might look odd to a modern carpenter, but the plane that the carpenter on the left is using would be instantly recognisable.

Pets

We know that medieval people used horses, oxen and other animals to work on the land. Wealthy people also hunted with specially trained dogs. These animals were useful, so were well treated. But did medieval people care about animals that had no use either for work or as food? Did they see animals as pets, as we do now, or did they simply see them as a source of food or as living tools to get a job done?

Bear baiting, painted in about 1400. In this sport, hunting dogs were made to attack a bear and people bet money on whether the dogs or the bear would survive the fight. Bulls were also baited in this way.

Every year on Shrove Tuesday, schoolboys bring fighting cockerels to school. They make these creatures fight all morning, making bets on which will win, then in the afternoon they play football. In winter, there is different sport in the morning on holy days. At this time, boars are set to fight, or bull and bears are baited.

Written in the medieval period by William FitzStephen.

Several popular sports involved violence between or against animals. Bulls and bears were baited. Cockfighting was also popular. Cockerels were also used as archery targets and even as targets for throwing stones at, or hitting with sticks. Most of these sports involved betting on the outcome and they were mostly played by men.

From _Daily Life in Chaucer's England_ by a modern historian.

Women, usually from the more important levels of society, often had pets. The pets gave the message that these women had the time to keep and play with pets and the money to feed them. They were a status symbol.

From _Pleasures and Pastimes in Medieval England_ by a modern historian.

The back of a royal travelling coach, painted in about 1400. The lady is being handed her lapdog.

Taking them with you?

In medieval times, important people had large brass plates engraved with a portrait or drawing put on to their tombstones or above their graves inside church. Medieval tomb brasses often show pets. The people, men and women, who had these images made obviously loved their pets. The brass of Thomas and Margaret de Freville of Little Shelford, made in 1410, shows Thomas with his sleek hunting dog, probably a greyhound, looking up at him devotedly. Two lapdogs, with bells around their collars, sit in the folds of Margaret's robe. In another brass, that of Sir Roger de Trumpington who died in 1289, Sir Roger's dog is playfully chewing the end of his sword scabbard!

Nuns' pets

There is a lot of evidence that nuns kept pets. They kept monkeys, birds, rabbits and squirrels, but the most common pets were dogs. Cats were not really kept as pets in the same way. Many homes had cats, but they were working cats, kept to kill the mice and rats. Most of the records we have of nuns' pets come from letters from the Church telling them that they should pay these creatures less attention, or keep them under better control. The Bishop of Winchester wrote to the abbess of Romsey in 1387:

Some of the nuns who join your order bring with them birds, rabbits, hounds and such like frivolous things, to which they pay more heed than to attending services, doing their duties and praying. This puts their souls in peril, so they may do so no longer.

Work it out!

'Medieval people were cruel to animals which were not working animals.'

1 a Which sources would you use to agree with this statement? Why?

  b Describe the sources which do not support this statement.

2 Did people make cockerels, bears and bulls fight just for the fun of seeing them die?

3 'Men treated non-working animals badly. Women kept them as pets.'

Do you think the information in this unit supports this statement, or is there evidence that it was not this simple?

Celebrating Christmas

The medieval period seems a very long time ago. If you travelled back to celebrate Christmas at that time you might be surprised to discover much that would be familiar today.

Similarities

- Holly, ivy and evergreen branches were used to decorate homes for Christmas.
- German Christmas celebrations included decorating an evergreen tree at this time; this may have happened in other European countries as well.
- Celebrations included dressing up, watching plays (usually funny, with lots of rough and tumble and mistaken identity) and playing games.
- People visited friends and relatives.
- Carols, Christmas songs written to dance to in non-religious celebrations, were written for church services for the first time.
- Christmas Day celebrations included a special dinner, although boar, not turkey, was eaten. Those who could not afford boar ate pies in the shape of a boar.

Differences

- Medieval Christmas celebrations were more tied to religious celebrations, and lasted longer. Some people celebrated the 12 days of Christmas, through to 6 January. But others celebrated in various ways all the way through to Candlemas, on 2 February.
- Although the feast of St Nicholas was in the Christmas period, he had not yet been turned into Santa Claus.
- People gave each other New Year presents, not Christmas presents.
- Mystery plays that told Bible stories were often performed in towns at Christmas. Some of these told the Christmas story, others told many of the well-known Bible stories from the Old and New Testaments.
- Some cathedral towns chose a boy-bishop to run the church for a week or two. Some small places allowed one of the villagers to rule as lord of the manor for a day. Rich people were expected to give 'hospitality', feed, even give overnight accommodation, to anyone who called on them, whether they were friends or strangers.

Robins were associated with Christmas long before Christmas cards were invented in Victorian times. This robin was painted in about 1400.

There was no dressing up, nor music, nor singing. There were no loud sports. Only board games, chess and card games were allowed.

A description, written in about 1450, of how the death of the master of the house affected the Christmas celebrations.

Work it out!

An anachronism is something which does not fit the period. A medieval person wearing a watch would be an anachronism.

Look at the medieval Christmas cartoon above. Write down all the anachronisms you can find, explaining why each one is an anachronism.

How important was the Church in people's lives in the Middle Ages?

It is almost impossible to stress how important the Church was in people's lives in the Middle Ages. It was the MOST important thing. The reason? If you did not do what the Church wanted; if you did not go to church every week; or if you did not believe what the Church said you went to hell. And hell was not a nice place; you did not want to go there! To remind you what hell was like, many churches had their own gruesome pictures of it painted on walls, carved in wood or stone or shown in stained glass windows.

A wall painting from a medieval country church showing Heaven and Hell. Top left are the scales of judgement, top right the angels and saints in Heaven trample on the devil, and on the central ladder bodies climb up to Heaven or tumble into Hell.

When William the Conqueror planned his conquest of England in 1066, he realised the importance of the Church in his efforts and he had the Pope's approval for his invasion. After his conquest William introduced the feudal system. You will know that this had the king at the top, followed by the barons, then their knights, with the peasants at the bottom.

What many people forget is that a major part of the system was the Church, which had its own ladder of power. The Church that everybody in England belonged to was the Catholic Church, led by the Pope in Rome.

In England the most senior members of the Church were the Archbishops, who appointed the bishops who in turn controlled the parish priests. This side of the feudal system was to control what the peasants thought and believed.

The Church was in control

Everybody was expected to go to church at least once every week. Everybody was expected to give 10 per cent of everything they owned to the Church. This was called a tithe. For the peasants this usually meant giving 10 per cent of everything they grew, as they did not have any money.

The Church controlled people's lives. They had to be baptised by the priest so that they would have a chance to go to heaven when they died. Everyone was married in church, usually in the doorway so that the whole village could see. Finally, in order to be able to go to heaven, they had to be buried in consecrated ground – that is the holy ground of the Church. Criminals suffered the terrible fate of being buried just by the side of the road, so that they could never reach paradise!

The church was the finest building in the village. Often it was the only building made of stone. It was bright and cheerful. The walls were covered in pictures showing stories from the Bible. The stained glass windows were inspiring, especially when the sun shone through.

It was a meeting place where the villagers could gossip. The church was also used for parties (called Church Ales) and often games and plays were performed there.

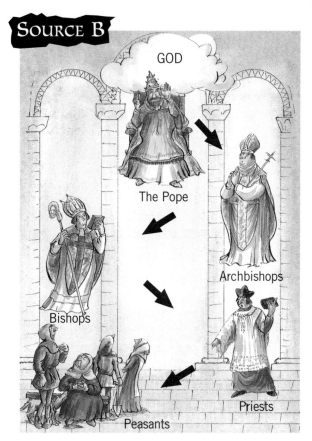

The organisation of control of the Church in England.

For the peasants, the Church provided the only days off from their work. Saints' days or Holy days were indeed holidays. There were over 100 Holy days (including Sundays).

The Church also provided the only help the peasants would receive if they were sick or ill. The monks in the monasteries were expected to nurse the sick. They were also expected to look after the old. They often provided education for the young. The only way to get on in medieval times was to be able to speak and write Latin, the language of the Church. Although ordinary peasants could not read or write, there was just a chance that a bright child might be adopted by the monks or priest and taught his letters. Any travellers could call into the monasteries for a bed and a meal, safe from fear of being attacked on the road. Finally, many peasants actually worked for the Church, farming the Church land.

Pilgrimages and superstition

Many people, including the peasants, went on pilgrimages to holy places. These could be places where saints were buried, or churches where relics were kept. It was very important to the people of the Middle Ages to go to a local cathedral to see or touch holy relics. A fragment of Jesus' cross, and teeth or bones from saints were typical relics found in many churches. However, if you put together all the bits of wood said to be from the cross you would have enough to make a dozen crosses! In France, two different cathedrals both claimed to have the head of John the Baptist.

The Bayeux Tapestry shows the solemn event of Harold swearing an oath of allegiance to Duke William on two chests of holy relics (see Source C). This would have been recognised as being of the greatest significance.

The people of the Middle Ages were very superstitious. They believed that God sent many signs to show His anger. Another famous scene from the Bayeux Tapestry shows the appearance of what is now known as Halley's Comet (see Source D). This was seen at the time to be a sign of God's anger against Harold for breaking his oath of allegiance to Duke William and taking the Crown of England.

The Church and the king

Throughout the Middle Ages, there was a battle between the king and the Church as to who was the most powerful. Obviously neither wanted to give in to the other. Henry II made his great friend Thomas Becket Archbishop of Canterbury. He hoped that Becket would make sure the Church agreed with the king's decisions. But Becket did not do so. Henry, who had a very bad temper, was overheard shouting to be 'rid of this troublesome priest'. Five of his knights promptly rode to Canterbury Cathedral and killed Becket.

Becket's burial site at Canterbury quickly became the most important shrine in England. The Pope made Becket a saint. More importantly for the Church, the king no longer tried to be more powerful than the Church. It would be during the Tudor period that that struggle would resume again.

SOURCE C

Harold swearing an oath of allegiance to Duke William on two chests of relics. A very important scene from the Bayeux Tapestry.

The English are seen pointing to the star (*stella*); one of them tells Harold, and below are the shadowy ships - of Duke William coming to claim his throne perhaps?

Challenge to the power of the Church

Not everyone inside the Church believed that the Pope and his bishops should have total power. Many priests were really only peasants who were just able to remember the Latin of the Mass. Many of them felt the same as the peasants. They objected to the bishops making lots of money whilst they remained poor. When the Peasants' Revolt (1381) took place many of the leaders were priests, and the most important of them was John Ball.

It was not only ordinary priests who felt sorry for the peasants and anger at the rich lifestyle of the bishops. John Wycliffe (died 1384) said that the higher members of the Church should have fewer riches and help the poor more. The followers of Wycliffe were called Lollards. John Wycliffe also said that the Bible should be in English. The Church was very worried about such ideas. So they banned them. Anybody following them would be *excommunicated*. This means that you were thrown out of the Church, which in the Middle Ages was a terrible thing. It meant that you were damned and would go to hell – to suffer for ever.

Work it out!

1 a Can you explain why pictures of hell were shown in most churches in the Middle Ages?

   b Can you explain why relics were so important to the people of the Middle Ages?

   c Can you explain why churches and monasteries were keen to have their own relics?

2 a List on a piece of paper the ways that the Church in the Middle Ages was so important in people's lives. Leave two lines between each point you have made.

   b Cut up your list so that each point is on a separate piece of paper.

   c Put the pieces of paper in order of importance, the most important point being at the top and the least important at the bottom.

   d Now write how important you think the Church was in people's lives, making sure you use your list to stress which were the most important things. Always give reasons for your answer.

What chance did people have of surviving medical treatment in the Middle Ages?

Today when we are ill we can expect to get better. For the people of the Middle Ages becoming ill or catching a disease was much more worrying. The reason? Medical treatment was usually more dangerous and life threatening than the original problem!

Will the baby live?

The problems began before they were even born. To survive childbirth was a feat in itself. It was a very dangerous and painful experience, both for mother and child. One in five pregnant women would die either during childbirth or soon after. For a baby to live beyond childbirth was also a matter of luck; over half of all babies born would die before they reached their first birthday. A large number died before reaching adulthood, and for those who did, the age of 40 was considered old.

Was country life or town life healthier?

For the villagers the main complaints were malnutrition (not getting enough food) and diseases caused by storing food over a long period of time. One such disease was St Anthony's Fire, which was said to lead to your arms and legs falling off! Living in the same house as their animals did not help the peasants to lead a healthy life, but with the fresh air and clean rivers, life in the country was better than life in the towns.

The towns were not clean places. Water was taken from wells, standpipes or the rivers, which were often also used as the local cesspits. At the beginning of the period there were no sewage systems; human waste and rubbish was simply thrown on to the street. Later on, cesspits were sometimes built below the houses, which then had to be emptied. It was a commonly held belief that the attendants of public latrines were immune from disease due to the smells coming from the toilets! Edward III did decree once that all the waste be removed from the streets of London, not for hygiene reasons but to get rid of the smell! Medieval people knew nothing about germs and the need for cleanliness. So what did they think were the causes of illness?

SOURCE A

An open toilet in a town. Notice the one above.

Why did people fall ill?

A commonly held belief was that worms caused disease. One cure for toothache involved heating your tooth with a candle till the worm fell out! Another idea why people became ill was based on the belief that people had four 'humours' in their bodies. These matched the elements earth, air, fire and water. Doctors believed that all four needed to be in balance in a patient. If you had too much, or too little, of one, then you became ill. Likewise, too much blood in the veins was often thought to cause illness and fever; the cure for this was to 'bleed' the patient (often making them very weak) by taking blood, sometimes with the use of leeches.

SOURCE B

A doctor bleeding a patient – from a 14th century manuscript.

The colour of a patient's urine could also point to the reasons for a patient's illness. This actually was not such a bad idea – if only the medieval doctors knew what they were looking for. It was certainly better than thinking that to drink your own urine could help cure you. Many medieval doctors believed this to be true.

Other doctors were more 'scientific'. They believed that people's illnesses were related to their star sign or what the planets were doing when they fell ill. There were certain days when they believed it impossible to cure a patient. A prominent French doctor 'proved' that the Black Death was caused by the close position of three planets – Saturn, Jupiter and Mars.

Even Galen, 'one of the most outstanding intellects of his age', believed that people fell ill of the plague as a result of something they had done, or eaten or drunk. Galen was very clear that a person's religious behaviour could influence their health. Certainly this was an idea believed by many, especially the Church itself, which encouraged the idea that being good would bring good health, whilst illness must be the result of 'bad' behaviour.

Treatments

If the doctors of the Middle Ages did not know what caused disease, were their treatments any good? Unfortunately not! However, there were many varied and interesting cures besides 'bleeding' patients, checking their urine, and checking their lifestyle.

Herbal remedies were frequently used by every sort of person. These were actually quite good, and many are still used today.

Remedies, advice and superstitions were passed down through families, and amongst the poor, superstitions were particularly powerful. One thing they believed was that scrofula, a disease of the skin, could be cured by the touch of the king. Generally the poor dealt with illnesses by themselves. The rich, though, could afford the best and most up to date treatment!

Amputations were a common remedy, but patients rarely survived. There were no anaesthetics or antiseptics. If they were lucky, they might be knocked out with too much wine or crushed poppy seeds (a form of heroin!). None of the instruments used would be sterilised, and the doctor would wear his ordinary clothes. Often the amputations would take place in a barber-surgeon's shop. This could be recognised by the pole outside the shop with the drying blood-filled towels on it. A barber-surgeon would train for seven years — learning the techniques of blood letting and on which 'days' not to treat a patient.

To help patients recover, doctors would recommend eating live spiders or animal dung.

Learning about illness

Physicians were scholars. They did go to university but they rarely saw a live patient to deal with or a dead body to practise on (the Church would not permit it). Galen had written many important books on the subject and his followers felt it was bad manners and disrespectful to challenge his ideas. Unfortunately, for his patients and theirs, he had based his ideas on what he had found out after cutting up pigs!

In fact it was the monks who had better training as medics than the doctors. They had constantly to deal with patients in the monasteries. A law passed in 1300 by the Church Council of Clermont banned all churchmen from being

Operating on a patient's head.

doctors or even practising medicine, so stopping the help the ill received. Fortunately, this did not last long. But the Church was always in favour of the idea that a person was ill because it was God's will.

Pope Boniface VIII said in 1300 that no bodies were to be mutilated. This was to stop relic hunters, but it also stopped any chance of anyone learning about the human body. Even the Medical Faculty of Paris was opposed to surgery. Any advance in medical knowledge was by trial and error.

However, if the Europeans had had any sense they would have seen what the Arabs were doing. The Arabs studied the patients. They developed drugs. They even had inspectors to check on the doctors and on the drugs they used. Arab hospitals had separate wards for different ailments. They had outpatients and even travelling clinics. All doctors had to pass exams. The most famous meeting between an Arab doctor and a European doctor resulted in the death of two patients! The Arab doctor had prescribed a new diet for a woman's bad head; and a poultice for a knight's bad leg. The European doctor was rude about the Arab's treatments. He amputated the knight's leg; the knight bled to death. He then took out the lady's brain and cleaned it! Not surprisingly, she died immediately. The Arab doctor could only watch in amazement.

By 1500, very little had improved. Henry VIII's first wife, Catherine, lost seven of their eight children. Henry's third wife, Jane, died soon after giving birth to their child.

SOURCE D

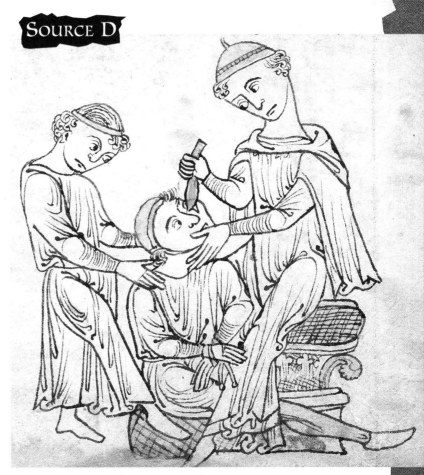

Operating on a patient's eye.

Work it out!

1 What reasons can you find to help prove that life in the towns was less healthy than in the villages?

2 a What were the humours?

  b Why did the doctors of the Middle Ages think they were so important?

3 Why would you rather be treated by a monk than by a surgeon or a doctor?

4 What chance did the people of the Middle Ages have of surviving any medical treatment that they might have?

5 If survival rates were so low, why did people bother to have medical treatment?

'Dangerous, uncomfortable and slow' – so why did people travel?

It is often said that the people of the Middle Ages rarely travelled from their villages, that they knew little of the outside world and cared even less. Up to a point this was true, but it is not the whole truth. Firstly, most people from the villages would be aware of their surrounding area for a radius of about ten miles. The local market town would usually be no more than ten miles away. Secondly, there was a wide range of other types of people in the Middle Ages who did travel.

Communication

Travel was actually more necessary in the Middle Ages than it is today. The people of the Middle Ages did not have telephones, televisions, faxes or the Internet. If you needed to talk to someone, to give him or her a message or an order, you had to go yourself or send a servant. The kings of England often had to send messengers to all parts of the kingdom. William the Conqueror sent officials all over the country to collect information about the possessions of his subjects for the Domesday Book, and bring it back to London.

Barons who received manors from William after the Conquest were given land in many different areas. This was done to help William keep control of the barons. It meant that the barons needed to travel to each of their manors every few weeks to order the running of the estate and to show the local villagers that they were in charge. It was important for the barons in their turn to keep control of the peasants (who might easily steal from the baron if he was away too long). The landowners would have to take many possessions with them on their travels to ensure that they were comfortable wherever they stayed, and to make sure they kept all their valuables safe.

SOURCE A

Manors usually had a permanent household to keep it running, and the more important servants would be expected to travel to different parts of the county to collect all the goods they needed. The most important of these were probably salt (for preserving food) and metal goods – things the manor could not provide for itself.

Markets

Travelling to the local market was the most important reason for everyone from landowner to peasant to take to the road. The market was the main place for the buying and selling and trading of animals, food, cloth, and many other items. Market day was also a very enjoyable and important occasion. It was a chance to meet old friends, to play games, to drink and to hear the news brought from further afield by pedlars and travelling traders. The pedlars went from village to village and the travelling traders toured the whole country and were always on the move.

At the markets and fairs there were often jugglers, musicians and acrobats. They would also visit the local castles and manor houses and were always welcome for their entertainment and news. There were also the high class traders – merchants of valuable goods who sold only the finest silks and spices. There were delivery men to help take goods to those who were unable to provide for themselves, or to travel. These regular travellers on the roads, who were used to journeying and knew their way, were useful companions for other travellers, who liked to walk with them as it was much safer than travelling alone.

Pilgrims

The travellers that you would be very likely to meet on your travels in the Middle Ages would be pilgrims or monks. The church encouraged people to travel by insisting that the monasteries look after travellers that came to their doors. Pilgrims would travel long distances to visit holy places such as Canterbury and to see holy relics. Monks would travel from monastery to monastery. Indeed, the few maps drawn at this time were maps of the routes to each monastery.

A travelling carriage for royal ladies, painted in about 1400.

Pilgrims outside Canterbury.

Runaway peasants

Occasionally, a peasant who had run away from his village might be seen travelling on his way to a large town. If he could hide in the town for a year and a day without being sent back to his village, then he would be a free person, no longer owned by the baron. There might also be drovers. These were men who took their cattle from place to place, especially on the Scottish borders. They would often travel hundreds of miles, similar to cowboys in the Wild West.

How did people travel?

Most of these travellers would travel either by foot, or, if they were rich enough, by horse. It was considered very unmanly to travel by wagon. Wagons were used only by women; the old and sick; or by prisoners, being taken to be hanged or imprisoned. In any case, wagons were very uncomfortable as they had hard seats and no springs.

Foot travellers would probably cover about 32-40 km a day. Travellers on horseback could do about 56 km a day. These journeys were very slow. They were even slower than during the Roman times. When Cicero (living in Rome) received 4 letters from Britain in the 1st century BC, they took about 27 days to reach him. By 1100, an important message from the Pope in Rome took 29 days to reach Canterbury. If it had been unimportant it could have taken up to seven weeks! At these speeds, it was obviously going to take more than a few days to travel any great distance.

Where to stay on the way?

For anyone wanting to travel further than they could walk or ride in a day, accommodation was important. The very rich and powerful would usually plan their journey many months in advance. They would send messengers beforehand to the noble houses along their route asking if (or stating that) they would be staying.

It would be a great honour for a lord of the manor to have the king or a bishop to stay and great feasts would be held in honour of their guests.

The poor would stay in a local monastery, where they would receive food and a bed, simple, plain but safe. Merchants would stay in travellers' inns. Here they would be able to get a meal (not usually very good) and a bed, which they might well have to share with other travellers. Inns were very dirty, travellers often complained of fleabites.

Travellers arriving at an inn (notice the sign). Inside, beds and bedrooms were shared at this inn.

Safety

Travel was dangerous. Robbers were a constant threat and worry. Edward I, in 1285, had to order his lords to clear all the bushes and trees for 60 metres either side of the main roads between market towns to stop robbers having a place to hide. The old Roman roads were used and these were protected by royal decree. This did not help the travellers on the other tracks. Wherever possible, travellers went in groups. Travellers were so pitied that they were prayed for regularly; they even had their own saint – St Christopher. The only guidance for which direction to travel came from local shepherds or farmers. It was during and after the Black Death that travelling became even more dangerous and lonely. There were fewer villagers out in the fields, and whole villages were deserted. It is no wonder that tales such as *Hansel and Gretel* and *Little Red Riding Hood* have their origins from this time. Travel was so dangerous, that some travellers wrote a will before they set off!

The condition of the roads was very often atrocious, with potholes, deep ruts, thick mud and overflowing streams being some of the frequent hazards. As many of the roads were merely well worn tracks, they became almost impassable in the winter months and were not often well maintained. Much of the level ground was marshy and waterlogged, whereas the hillsides were covered in vast stretches of woodland. In 1499, near Aylesbury, a glove-merchant fell into a two-metre hole, which he thought was just a puddle, and drowned! In fact, a local miller had dug the hole to look for clay. The miller was not punished, as it was agreed that he could not have got the clay anywhere else!

The word 'journey' comes from the French word *la journée*, which means 'day'. Obviously, many journeys took longer than a day, but perhaps the name stuck because it was really only safe to travel for one day and no more! The fact is that the people of the Middle Ages did travel, despite all the hardships and problems. Indeed, it was an important part of their culture: a chance to acquire new goods; to see people and events that they otherwise would miss; or for the rich, a chance to keep control of the people that they ruled.

Work it out!

1 Why did people in the Middle Ages have to travel?

2 Can you think of a method of transport not mentioned in the text that some people in the Middle Ages might have used?

3 Where did different travellers stay on their travels?

4 The title of this chapter says that travel in the Middle Ages was 'dangerous, uncomfortable and slow'. Would you agree with this statement?

Note To answer this question you should break your answer into three sections:

Section 1 should start: I think travel was/was not dangerous because.......

Section 2 should then start: I think travel was/was not uncomfortable because.......

Section 3 should then start: I think travel was/was not slow because......

All work and no play? Was this true for the people of the Middle Ages?

It is a popular myth that the life of the people of the Middle Ages was one of constant drudgery and hardship – they worked, went to church and waited for death. This could not be further from the truth. People in the Middle Ages did have free time, and many of the things that you enjoy doing, were enjoyed by the people of the Middle Ages.

The rich at play

At the beginning of the medieval period, hunting was the main activity for the rich, and it served the dual purpose of maintaining their fighting skills and being enjoyable. When Harold Godwinson was shipwrecked in Normandy before 1066, he and William of Normandy went hunting and hawking. When William conquered England, he took control of huge stretches of forests for his own personal hunting. Chasing and killing fast and agile animals and birds was good practice for fighting other knights, and was besides an exciting, skilful and very popular sport.

In times of peace, and during the cold winter months, the rich demanded entertainment in their castles. Travelling acrobats and jesters were hired to perform in the feasting hall. Minstrels would sing popular songs, tell long stories in verse, or sing ballads. As time went on, the rich read more. They started to collect books and pictures, helped by the introduction of the printing press in 1476 by William Caxton. The rich began to write letters. Some of these have been published in modern times, such as *The Paston Letters*. They give a wonderful picture of the social life in this period.

SOURCE A

OLO DVX: ANGLORVM: ETSVI MILITES: EQVI TANT: AD BOS

Harold and his soldiers ride to the coast. Harold has a hawk on his wrist and hounds run in front. From the Bayeux Tapestry.

A king plays chess with one of his courtiers.

SOURCE B

Girls learnt how to embroider, sing and dance. By the 1400s music was also becoming very popular. Knights returning from the Crusades brought back new games from the East; among the most popular were chess, draughts and backgammon. These were games of strategy and tactics.

Jousting

However, the most serious and time-consuming activity for men was, from childhood on, to train for war. Fighting, on foot or on horseback, with all the different weapons, was a most important skill. A knight's role in society was to fight loyally for his master. By being loyal and trustworthy a knight earned all his lands and privileges. When the knights were not fighting, they needed to train by fighting mock battles. Slowly these developed into tournaments, with jousts between two knights charging at each other with blunt lances. The change was, in part, due to the high numbers of deaths in the mock battles!

These tournaments soon became major events, full of pomp and glamour. The jousts were also the first sports to have rigidly defined rules. The knights could not only show off their fighting skills but also impress the ladies. Edward III was keen to set up tournaments. This was due to the people's interest in the French wars. Tournaments were never so popular as during the Hundred Years War.

What about ordinary people?

It was not only the rich who enjoyed themselves. Ordinary people watched and bet on bear baiting, cock fighting and wrestling matches. They gambled, played dice and cards. They also loved to drink; ale was cheap and many got drunk. Market days offered lots of entertainment – jugglers, acrobats, dancing bears, and puppet shows might all arrive, and the travelling fairs were full of all these and more. Children had their own games such as hoops, skipping ropes and pogo sticks. Shows like Punch and Judy were very popular.

Children at a Punch and Judy show, probably from the 14th century.

Plays and processions

The town guilds would sometimes perform 'miracle' or 'mystery' plays. These plays were based on Bible stories that were somehow related to the guild's own craft. For example, ship builders would retell the story of Noah and his Ark. The plays were often seen as a way the guild could show off to the public, although they cost a lot of money and some of the poorer craft guilds tried to avoid doing them. They were always great occasions; initially they were performed in the church, but as the audience and interest grew, the plays had to be performed in the street. The guilds also held colourful processions through the streets with many people in fancy dress. The procession would start at the church, where prayers were said, and then go on to a great banquet.

Medieval football

One of the most popular sports, then as now, was a version of football. A pig's bladder would be blown up and then kicked around. The rules varied in different parts of the country, but a popular game was one village against another village.

The ball was placed between the two villages and the object was to get the ball to the opponent's village green first. It did not matter how it got there. Or who you had to hurt to get it there! It was a very rough and violent game involving almost all of the men from the village.

SOURCE D

All and everyone is forbidden to take part in the hurling of stones, handball, football, hockey, coursing, cockfighting or such idle games of no value. On holidays all fit men must practise archery.

A statement by Edward III to make men train for battle.

One of Edward III's main concerns was to train skilled archers. They played a crucial part in the wars against the French. The fact that he issued a proclamation against sports and 'idle games' (see Source D) meant that these sports must have been very popular, too popular in fact. This was not just amongst the peasants either. Even the monks and nuns were keen to have a good time (see Source E).

57

Monks and nuns playing bat and ball.

Enjoy today – you may die tomorrow!

Sudden death was a very real fear, and spurred people on to live life to the full. When the Black Death struck, the fear of catching the plague must have encouraged many people to indulge themselves even more. People overate, overdrank and over-indulged themselves in many other pleasures that were normally frowned upon. This was especially so of the young, so not much different from today! What was also similar to today was the way that the tournaments led to problems of public order; entire towns would need to come under the control of the law keepers. Also, the more popular jousters would become sporting heroes, the pin-ups of their day.

Work it out!

1 List as many pastimes as you can that the people of the Middle Ages took part in.

2 Why do you think that Edward III was very concerned about the fact that his subjects preferred football to archery?

3 Produce a poster advertising a local tournament. Remember to stress the excitement, the risks and the bloodthirsty nature of the event. Make up some names of the stars of the jousts!

4 Your history teachers tell you that the people of the Middle Ages lived a miserable life. Prepare a speech that will prove them wrong. Include as much evidence as you can.

'Unloved, unwanted and unlikely to live!' Is this how it was for medieval children?

Life for children in the Middle Ages was very hard and many did not survive. It is probable that half of all the babies born died before they were a year old, and thereafter only one in ten would reach the age of ten. Mothers would hope to give birth to many children knowing that not all would be likely to survive.

The care of young children

It was the practice in the Middle Ages to swaddle your children, which meant wrapping a baby in a bandage-like material from head to toe. This was probably done for two main reasons. Firstly, people believed that a child's limbs needed to be straightened out. Secondly, it allowed a child to be left unattended while the rest of the family were at work, because it couldn't move. Some people even hung babies on hooks to keep them out of harm's way!

The biggest fear was that unattended children might roll into the fire that was keeping them warm. If this happened, the family could be punished; it wasn't seen as an accident. Preachers told their parishioners to tie their cots securely and not to leave young children unattended, especially near boiling water or open fires. Laws and sermons about such dangers suggest they were common. With small houses full of people and animals, however, accidents must have been frequent.

SOURCE A

This late medieval woodcut shows death taking a young child from a poor house. Just because young children were more likely to die then than now does not mean that the family were not upset when it happened.

Children at work

Peasant children began work as young as possible. At the age of four or five boys could scare away the birds from the fields, and remove the stones in front of the plough. As they got older they could look after the sheep and pigs, collect wood for the fire and any materials such as clay and reeds that were needed for house building. Girls would learn from their mothers how to cook, make and repair clothes, look after the animals as well as their younger brothers and sisters. They would also learn how to brew beer, make cheese and spin; all considered women's work.

Training

Some children of richer people were sent away at the age of seven to be looked after by another family. This led one Italian visitor to England to state that 'the English do not like their own children'. Parents would send their own children away, only to receive someone else's child in return. It was felt easier to control a stranger's child than your own. Parents of daughters would try to ensure that their daughter went to a household of slightly higher social status, in the hope that this might result in a marriage between the two families.

Sons of merchants, craftsmen and traders would be expected to follow their father's trade, but the family would pay another master to teach and look after their child. This 'apprenticeship' would last for seven years. During this time the master would feed, clothe and train the apprentice who would live in the master's house as part of the family. Then the young man would go and work for different masters, and would be known as a journeyman. Finally, after another seven years, or more, the journeyman would be asked to produce a masterpiece and could then become a master. It was very unusual for girls to do this; if a woman was in business, she was most likely a widow who had taken over from her dead husband.

SOURCE C

A peasant woman stirs the pot while the child works the bellows.

Education

If parents had hopes that their son might do even better than learn the family trade, they might send him to the local grammar school. These were set up and paid for by local wealthy men. The name 'grammar' school comes from the fact that the only real subject learnt was Latin grammar. These schools were not much like ours today. Lessons began at sunrise and would last for up to nine hours. It was very unlikely that the pupils would see a book, as all lessons had to be learnt by heart. Also parents expected their children to be beaten!

Girls were usually taught at home or in a nunnery. They might be taught to read the Bible and prayer book, also to sing, to play a musical instrument, if there was one, and how to sew. Management of the household was also important – the preserving of fruits, the drying of herbs, and the making of many things, from medicines to soap and candles. The richer girls might be taught how to play chess, to hunt with a hawk and to retell interesting stories.

A medieval painting of a guild master.

The son of a rich baron would usually be sent to live with another noble family from the age of seven. He would be a page boy, and would be taught how to behave, how to clean his master's armour, how to help his master to get dressed and how to serve his master with food. He might also be taught to read and write. At 14, he would become a squire and begin his training to become a knight.

To ensure that the children knew how to behave in someone else's house there were many rules to learn.

Here are some of them:

1. When eating have clean hands.
2. Don't eat too quickly.
3. Don't spit out any food you have in your mouth.
4. Don't pick your ears or nose.
5. Don't drink and eat at the same time.
6. Don't pick your teeth with your knife.
7. Don't throw bones on the floor.
8. Don't spit into the basin you wash in.

SOURCE E

Lac pueroz. M. holti Mylke for chyldren.

Children did not always mind their manners just because books told them to. An abbot from the time was found to complain that whatever he did he could do nothing with the children. He said day and night he would tell them off and beat them, yet they became worse and worse every day. A colleague did reply that it was not so godly to be against children. He suggested that the children be treated in the same way as he would like himself to be treated. His advice was: if you want to see your boys have good manners you should not just beat them but also give them fatherly kindness and pity. What good advice!

Work it out!

1 Why was a child considered fortunate to reach his/her tenth birthday?

2 What did the children do in the following households:

   a A peasant's household?

   b A tradesman's household?

   c A baron's household?

3 To a child what was the importance of reaching the following age:

   a Seven?

   b Fourteen?

   c Twenty-one?

4 Is it true that children of the Middle Ages were 'unloved, unwanted, and unlikely to reach the age of ten'? Remember to include evidence in your answer to cover both sides of the argument.

Woodcut showing a schoolroom. The master has his birch stick ready. The pupils have books of their own, but this was unusual in medieval schools.

Glossary

amputation the removal of a limb, normally an arm or a leg, in an operation.

apprentice a person who is learning a trade by living and working for several years with someone who is already qualified in that trade.

archer a soldier who fired bows and arrows.

backgammon game brought back from the Arabs during the Crusades. It is a game of skill using dice and counters.

carpenter a person who makes things from wood.

chronicle a record of events or an account of the time.

chronology the order in which events happen over time.

citizen a person who lives in a town.

convent a group of people who devoted their lives to religion. We now use the word to describe the building in which nuns live.

courtier a person who lived and sometimes worked with the king or queen.

craftsman a person who is trained in making a particular thing, for example: shoemakers, potters, bakers.

cross-referencing checking historical facts given in at least two pieces of evidence.

Domesday Book William the Conqueror sent out his officials to collect the details of all the possessions of his subjects. All the information was stored in two books called *The Domesday Book*.

fish-pond a man-made pond or set of ponds, used for breeding fish to eat.

freeman a person who can own his own land and house, rather than being given them by the lord of the manor in return for work.

garderobe a medieval toilet.

glazier a person who works with glass, mostly making windows.

heir a person who inherits another person's land and possessions after their death.

humours the 'four humours' theory of medicine said that the human body was made up of four elements: earth, air, fire and water. Each of these controlled a different substance in the body: blood, black bile, yellow bile and phlegm. Depending on the time of year, these elements could get out of balance and produce an 'ill humour' – too much of one of the substances in the body. This made a person ill.

journeyman an apprentice who has learned his trade, and travels to try to sell his goods in different markets. When he is ready, he can make his masterpiece. This is to show off his skill. If the local craft guild thinks it is good enough, and if he has enough money to join the guild, he can become a craftsman.

Lord of the Manor the person who controls all the land in a village or group of villages, who is given the land by the king.

manor a village or group of villages all controlled by the same lord.

manor court the court which settles all village disputes in one manor. It is run by the lord of the manor, or someone he chooses to do the job. If a jury is needed, they are chosen from the manor.

manuscript a handwritten document.

mason a person who builds things from stone.

master mason a skilled mason, who runs big building projects (like castles) and organises other masons and all the other workers on the site.

medieval an expression used to describe the period of history from about 1000 to 1500.

merchant a trader who buys and sells goods (such as silk or spices), sometimes with traders from abroad.

monastery the place where monks lived. Here they would pray, meditate, teach and look after the needy.

mourning the expression of great sadness following the death of someone.

oath of allegiance this is a very solemn and sacred undertaking. A knight would pledge his friendship and loyalty to another person (the king) on some holy relics. It would be dishonourable to break the oath.

pedlar a travelling seller who had small items to sell. He would travel the country, taking with him news and gossip.

pilgrimage a journey to a place which has special religious importance.

Poll Tax the first tax that everyone, rich or poor, had to pay. It was introduced in 1377. Earlier taxes had been taken from well-off people.

Pope the head of the Roman Catholic Church, a very powerful and influential man.

privy a medieval toilet that was a seat or set of seats fixed over a deep pit, which had to be emptied regularly.

relics these were items of clothing, ornaments or even parts of a person's body, believed to belong to very religious people. Pilgrims travelled miles to pray to them.

saint a person that the Church has said did something especially holy. This could be someone who lived a very good life, but was most often someone killed for their religious beliefs.

shrine a place that is special to a saint (such as the place they died) or has something that belonged to a saint kept in it.

sources of evidence information telling us about the past.

stained glass pictures made of coloured glass, usually found in the windows of churches.

tournament a sporting occasion where different knights would compete against each other in a series of trials of strength.

villein a person who is given his house and land by the lord of the manor in return for work. He cannot leave the manor without permission from the lord.